Flavors of the World – Croatia

Over 25 Recipes to Guide You Through Croatian Cooking

BY: Nancy Silverman

COPYRIGHT NOTICES

My Heartfelt Thanks and A Special Reward for Your Purchase!

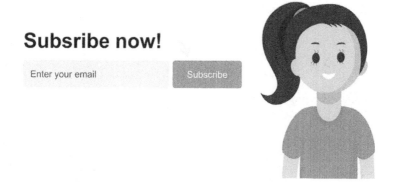

https://nancy.gr8.com

My heartfelt thanks at purchasing my book and I hope you enjoy it! As a special bonus, you will now be eligible to receive books absolutely free on a weekly basis! Get started by entering your email address in the box above to subscribe. A notification will be emailed to you of my free promotions, no purchase necessary! With little effort, you will be eligible for free and discounted books daily. In addition to this amazing gift, a reminder will be sent 1-2 days before the offer expires to remind you not to miss out. Enter now to start enjoying this special offer!

Table of Contents

The Influence of the Croatian Cuisine

When you first begin to enjoy Croatian cuisine, you will not necessarily think that it is comprised of different cuisines. The truth of the matter is the Croatian cuisine is made up of both Eastern European Cuisine and Southern European cuisine. This is what gives Croatian food its delicious and exotic taste that many people cannot resist. In this section you will learn more about Croatian cuisine so that you can understand exactly where the different blends of flavor come from.

(1) Italian Influence

One of the many places that Croatian food is influenced from is Italy. This is because Italy is in close proximity to Croatia and you will find that many Croatian dishes often originates from Italy. Whether it is homemade pasta, homemade pizza or gelato you can rest assure that you can find Italian dishes anywhere within Croatia.

(2) Coastal Condiments

Another aspect of Croatian cuisine that you need to understand is its condiments. Condiments that are used with the Croatian Cuisine is influenced by coastal regions around the area such as the beach or islands. With that being said most of the condiments that you will find being used for Croatian dishes include olive oil and salt. Olive oil in itself is able to influence the taste of many Croatian dishes to the point that it is what makes it. The same thing goes for salt, especially sea salts. Sea salt is not a precious commodity as it used to be, but it is still an ingredient that is used to help give Croatian dishes its unique flavor.

(3) Seafood Influence

Another thing that you will automatically recognize about this cuisine is the abundance of seafood in Croatian dishes. It is so important to the Croatian cuisine that many restaurants will only serve this within Croatia. Most of the fish that you can find are fresh fish that are found along the coastline whether that is fresh salmon, tuna or even decadent oysters. If seafood is not your thing, then Croatian dishes may not be the best option for you.

(4) Pag Cheese

This delicacy is something that makes people smile from ear-to-ear. Before nearly every meal you can find this type of cheese being served up. This cheese is unique in flavor thanks to Croatia's salt production center, so it is a great dish to have if you are looking for something that is delicious with a nice smelling aroma.

(5) The Influence of Meat

If seafood is not your thing you can find plenty of meat options available to you within the Croatian Cuisine. You can find classics such as chicken, veal, beef, lamb and turkey. However, one of the most popular dishes often served with Croatian Cuisine is the Zagorski Strukli. It is a cheese-based dish that is layered with cheese and traditional beef.

(6) Wine

What is a delicious Cuisine without its own pairing of delicious drinks? Within this cuisine you will find a robust wine industry, hence why wine is one of the most popular drinks served in the country today. You can go find a variety of wines there that will fit your specific tastes. You can find various wines that are influenced from traditional Italian wines and you will surely not be disappointed with them. With that said I highly recommend pairing a simple pinot Gregio or sweet tasting red wine with most of the dishes you make to really make it delicious.

(7) Desserts

What cuisine doesn't include delicious desserts to end off every meal? Some of the desserts that you will find with Croatian Cuisine are unlike some that you have ever tried before. Whether you love to enjoy delicious plums with ice cream or enjoy a traditional cake, you can always rest assured that you can find your favorite dessert dish to satisfy your strongest sweet tooth.

(8) Caffeine

Just like many European countries today Croatia is renowned for its Cafe industry. There is absolutely nothing better than enjoying a nice cup of coffee with a delicious dessert dish or while you were talking amongst friends in the neighborhood. There many different types of coffee that you can enjoy but the most popular one often served up is a simple espresso. With this said you need to keep in mind that some of the coffee that is often served in Croatia are one of the strongest that you will ever find so make sure you never drink a cup right before bedtime as it will keep you up throughout the entire night.

25 Delicious Croatian Recipes

(1) Croatian Style Fish Stew

This is the perfect dish to make for any lover of seafood. It is packed with many seafood favorites such as Sea Bass, shrimp and Monkfish. It is so delicious I know you won't be able to get enough of it.

Serving Sizes: 8 Servings

Preparation Time: 35 Minutes

List of Ingredients:

- 1 Cup of Parsley Leaves, Fresh and Packed
- ½ Cup of Olive2 Oil, Extra Virgin Variety
- ¼ Cup of Lemon Juice, Fresh
- 14 Cloves of Garlic, Sliced Thinly
- Dash of Salt and Pepper, For Taste
- 1 Pound of Monkfish Fillets, With Pin Bones Removed
- 1 Pound of Seabass Fillets, With Pin Bones Removed
- 10 Ounces of Shrimp, Medium in Size, Raw, Peeled, Deveined and with Tails Removed
- 6 Langoustines, Unpeeled, Raw and with Heads On

- 1 Pound of Yukon Potatoes, Peeled and Sliced Thinly
- 2 Leeks, Small in Size, White and Green Parts Halved and Sliced Thinly
- 1 Red Onion, Large in Size and Sliced Thinly
- 1 Yellow Onion, Large in Size and Sliced Thinly
- 1 Cup of White Wine, Dry Variety
- 1, 28 Ounce Can of Tomatoes, Whole, Peeled and Crushed

||||||||||||||||||||||||||||||||||||||||||||||||||||||

Methods:

1. First place your parsley, half of your oil, fresh lemon juice, half of your garlic, dash of salt and pepper into a food processor. Process on the highest setting until smooth in consistency. Transfer this mixture into a large sized bowl.

2. Add your fish fillets, shrimp and langoustines into the same bowl. Toss thoroughly to combine and allow to chill in your fridge for the next 10 minutes.

3. Next grease a large sized Dutch oven with some oil.

4. Add in your remaining garlic, potatoes, leeks and onions into a large sized bowl. Spread this mixture into the bottom of your pan.

5. Add in your remaining oil, wine and tomatoes into it.

6. Then remove your shrimp and langoustines from your marinade. Set this mixture aside and place at least 1/3 of your shrimp over the top.

7. Repeat these layers and add in at least 1 cup of water. Allow to come to a boil before reducing the heat to low.

8. Continue to cook until your vegetables are tender to the touch. This should take at least 12 to 15 minutes.

9. Add your shrimp and langoustines into it. Cover and continue to cook for the next 5 minutes.

10. Remove from heat and serve while still piping hot. Enjoy!

(2) Croatian Style Fishy Packed Stew

Here is yet another fish stew recipe that I know you won't be able to get enough of. It contains three different types of fish that any fish lover will fall in love with. For the tastiest results I highly recommend making this dish with the freshest fish you can find.

Serving Sizes: 6 Servings

Preparation Time: 35 Minutes

List of Ingredients:

- 3.3 Pounds of Fish, Ocean, Scorpion Variety, Reef and Rockfish Variety
- ¼ Cup of Olive Oil, Extra Virgin variety
- 4 Tablespoon of Vinegar, White in Color
- 6 Cloves of Garlic, Thinly Sliced
- ½ Bunch of Parsley, Flat Leaf Variety and Roughly Chopped
- 3 Onions, Large in Size and Finely Chopped
- ½ Cup of Tomatoes, Finely Chopped
- Dash of Salt and Pepper, For Taste
- 2 ½ Cups of Water, To Cover
- 12 Mussels, Cleaned and Debearded
- 6 Scampi

IIIIIIIIIIIIIIIIIIIIIIIIIIIIIIIIIIIIIIIIIIIIIIIIIIIII

Methods:

1. Use a large sized saucepan and heat up your oil over medium heat. Once the oil is hot enough add in your garlic and onion. Cook for the next 5 to 10 minutes.

2. After this time add in your tomatoes and a touch of water. Cook for the next 10 minutes.

3. Then season your dish with some salt. Add to your saucepan. Mix thoroughly to combine.

4. Add in enough water to cover your fish.

5. Pour in your vinegar and dash of pepper. Reduce the heat to low and allow to simmer for the next 20 minutes before adding your scampi into your saucepan.

6. Continue to cook for the next 5 minutes. Remove from heat.

7. Season with another touch of salt and pepper and serve while still piping hot. Enjoy.

(3) Croatian Style Sausages

This tasty Croatian dish is absolutely delicious, especially if you serve it straight off of the grill. They are incredibly easy to make and can become quite an addictive treat within your household.

Serving Sizes: 4 Servings

Preparation Time: 2 Hours and 20 Minutes

List of Ingredients:

- 4 Pounds of Pork, Lean
- 2 Onions, Medium in Size and Minced
- 3 Cloves of Garlic, Minced
- 1 Tablespoon of Sea Salt, For Taste
- 1 Tablespoon of Black Pepper, For Taste
- 4 Tablespoon of Paprika, Hungarian Style and Hot
- 4 Tablespoon of Paprika, Hungarian Style and Sweet in taste
- 6 Tablespoon of Parsley, Fresh and Minced
- 3 ½ Tablespoon of Olive Oil, Extra Virgin Variety
- 2 ½ Tablespoon of Baker's Style Baking Powder
- ¾ Cup of Water Carbonated Variety

||||||||||||||||||||||||||||||||||||||||||||||||||

Methods:

1. First place all of your ingredients into a large sized bowl.

2. Mix several times until a pasty mixture begins to form.

3. Cover your bowl with some plastic wrap and place into your fridge to chill for the next 2 hours.

4. After this time shape your mixture using your hands into small sized logs.

5. Add in some oil to a large sized skillet and set over medium heat. Once your oil is hot enough add in your sausages and cook until seared and fully cooked on all sides.

6. Remove from heat and serve whenever you are ready.

(4) Classic Croatian Style Rice and Beans

This is a tasty Croatian style recipe to make if you are looking for a dish to accompany your next Croatian meal. It is relatively easy to prepare and is the perfect way to end off your busiest day in a delicious way.

Serving Sizes: 6 Servings

Preparation Time: 35 Minutes

List of Ingredients:

- 2 Liters of Chicken Stock, Homemade Preferable
- 1 ½ Cups of Rice, Arborio or Carnaroli Style
- 1 Onion, Large in Size and Finely Diced
- 1 Clove of Garlic, Finely Diced
- 1 Carrot, Fresh and Finely Diced
- Dash of Olive Oil, Extra Virgin variety
- 1/3 Cup of Parmesan Cheese, Freshly Grated
- ¼ Cup of Butter, Soft
- 1/3 Cup of Wine, White and Dry Variety
- ¾ Cup of Peas, Fresh

- 5 Rashers of Pancetta, Finely Diced

IIIIIIIIIIIIIIIIIIIIIIIIIIIIIIIIIIIIIIIIIIIIIIIIIIIII

Methods:

1. Heat up a large sized skillet placed over low to medium heat. Once your skillet is hot enough add in your oil, garlic, onions, fresh carrots and pancetta. Cook for the next 5 minutes or until your onions are translucent.

2. Add in your rice and stir thoroughly to coat in your oil. Continue to cook for an additional 30 seconds.

3. After this time add in your wine and stir continuously until it evaporates.

4. Add in your stock and stir thoroughly to mix. Cover and cook for the next 15 minutes or until your rice is fully cooked through.

5. During the last 5 minutes of cooking, add in your peas and stir again to incorporate.

6. Remove from heat and add in your butter and parmesan cheese. Stir thoroughly to combine and allow to sit for the next 10 minutes. Serve while still warm and enjoy.

(5) Simple Croatian Tossed Salad

This delicious summer time salad is one that you can find in nearly every Croatian home or restaurant today. What really makes this dish pop is the vinegar that you will be using as it is one of the most important ingredients in this dish.

Serving Sizes: 3 Servings

Preparation Time: 10 Minutes

List of Ingredients:

- ¾ Cup of Tomatoes, Fresh
- ½ Cup of Green Peppers, Finely Diced
- ½ Cup of Cucumbers, Fresh
- ½ Cup of Onions, Optional and Finely Diced
- 2 Tablespoon of Vinegar
- 1 Tablespoon of Olive Oil, Extra Virgin Variety
- Dash of Salt and Pepper, For Taste

||||||||||||||||||||||||||||||||||||||||||||||||||||||

Methods:

1. The first thing that you will want to do is chop your veggies into small sized pieces.

2. Then add to a large sized bowl and drizzle your vinegar over the top.

3. Season with a dash of salt and pepper.

4. Allow to sit in your fridge for at least 30 minutes.

5. After this time remove and serve while cold.

(6) Savory Peach Cake Recipe

This savory Croatian dish, also known as Breskvice is a traditional dish made during many Croatian family events. It is so delicious even the pickiest of eaters can't turn this dish away.

Serving Sizes: 6 Servings

Preparation Time: 1 Hour and 20 Minutes

Ingredients for Your Peach Cakes:

- 6 Eggs, Large in Size and Separated
- ¾ Cup of Sugar, Confectioner's Variety
- 1 Tablespoon of Sugar, Vanilla Flavored
- 4 Ounces of Butter, Soft and Unsalted Variety
- 2 teaspoon of Peach Brandy, Optional
- 1 Lemon, Juice Only
- 2 ½ Cups of Flour, Pastry Variety
- 2 teaspoon of Baker's Style Baking Powder

Ingredients for Your Filling:

- 2 teaspoon of Cocoa, Powdered Variety
- 2 teaspoon of Rum, Dark in Color
- 2 Cups of Jam, Peach or Apricot Flavored
- 1 to 2 Tablespoon of Milk, Whole
- 1 ½ Cups of Walnuts, Ground Variety

Ingredients for Your Decoration:

- ¼ Cup of Water, Warm
- Dash of Food Coloring, Red in Color
- ¼ Cup of Brandy, Peach Variety
- Dash of Food Coloring, Yellow in Color
- ½ Cup of Sugar, White and Coarse in Texture

||||||||||||||||||||||||||||||||||||||||||||||||||||

Methods:

1. The first thing that you will want to do is make your peach cakes. To do this use a large sized bowl and beat your egg yolks, confectioner's sugar and vanilla flavored sugar together until it is frothy in texture.

2. Then add in your brandy, soft butter and fresh lemon juice. Beat with an electric mixer until evenly combined.

3. Use a second large sized mixing bowl and whip your eggs whites with an electric mixer until stiff to the touch.

4. Take at least a quarter of your egg white mixture and fold into your first mixture until evenly mixed together.

5. Use a third mixing bowl and whisk together your baker's style baking powder and flour until evenly combined. Sift into your batter with your egg whites and stir gently to combine.

6. Cover your mixture and place into your fridge to chill for at least 1 hour.

7. During this time preheat your oven to 350 degrees.

8. While your oven is heating up use at least 1 teaspoon of your batter and roll it into a ball using your hands. Place onto a baking sheet and repeat until all of your batter has been used up.

9. Place into your oven to bake for the next 6 to 8 minutes or until light golden brown in color. After this time remove and allow to cool completely.

10. Once your balls are cooled, cut a small circle out from the bottom of your ball and scoop out the insides, making sure to preserve them in a separate bowl.

11. Next make your filling. To do this place your cake insides into a food processor along with your cocoa, dark rum, jam and your whole milk. Process on the highest setting until thoroughly mixed.

12. Transfer this mixture into a medium sized bowl and add in your walnuts and remaining milk. Stir thoroughly until your filling is moist to the touch.

13. Fill the holes of your cake balls with this filling and repeat until all of your filling has been used.

14. Add at least ¼ cup of water into a small sized bowl and add in your red food coloring. Mix well to combine.

15. Add your peach brandy to another small sized bowl along with your yellow food coloring and stir well to mix. Add your sugar into another small sized bowl.

16. Take each of your cakes at least halfway into each food coloring bowl and roll in your sugar.

17. Place onto a baking sheet to dry completely. Repeat until all of your cake balls have been coated. Serve whenever your balls are dry. Enjoy.

(7) Traditional Pasticada

This traditional Croatian dish is served in many traditional restaurants and made in many homes. It is a dish that is usually served with delicious gnocchi. Feel free to serve this up during the New Year to bring in the new year in a delicious way.

Serving Sizes: 6 Servings

Preparation Time: 16 Hours and 20 Minutes

List of Ingredients:

- 3 to 4 Pounds of Beef Round
- 5 Cloves of Garlic, Finely Sliced
- 4 Ounces of Bacon, Cut into Small Sized Pieces
- 4 Cups of Vinegar, Wine Variety
- ½ Cup of Olive Oil, Extra Virgin Variety
- 1 Cup of Broth, Vegetable Variety and Homemade Preferable
- 3 Onions, Cut into Quarters
- 2 Carrots, Fresh, Peeled and Finely Diced
- 1 Celery Root, Peeled and Cut into Quarters
- 1 Parley Root, Peeled and Cut into Quarters

- 1 Tablespoon of Flour, All Purpose Variety
- 4 Cloves, Whole
- 2 Tablespoon of Tomato Paste
- 1 Bay Leaf, Dried
- ½ Cup of Wine, Dessert Variety
- 1 Tablespoon of Sugar, White
- ½ Cup of Wine, Dry and Red Variety
- 4 Prunes
- 1 Pound of Gnocchi
- Dash of Parmesan Cheese, Optional
- ½ Bunch of Parsley, Fresh and Roughly Chopped
- Dash of Salt and Pepper, For Taste

||||||||||||||||||||||||||||||||||||||||||||||||||

Methods:

1. First pierce your meat with a sharp knife and add your cloves, garlic and bacon into these slits.

2. Then place your meat into a large sized baking dish.

3. Cover with some vinegar and cover with some plastic wrap. Place into your fridge to marinate overnight.

4. The next day remove your meat from the vinegar and remove the bacon and garlic. Set the bacon and garlic aside.

5. Place your meat into a large sized Dutch oven.

6. Dust the beef with some flour and add in your olive oil.

7. Cook over medium to high heat. Cook your meat on all sides for the next 8 to 10 minutes or until thoroughly brown in color. Once brown remove from your Dutch oven.

8. Add your reserved bacon, garlic and onion in the same pot for the next 5 minutes or until translucent.

9. After this time add your meat back into your Dutch oven. Add in your broth and continue to cook for the next 6 to 8 minutes.

10. Add in your tomato paste, both wines and sugar. Stir thoroughly to combine.

11. Reduce the heat to low and cover. Cook for the next 3 hours or until your meat is tender to the touch.

12. Halfway during the cooking process add in your prunes and bay leaf.

13. Once cooked remove your meat and slice into thin slices.

13. Add your juice and veggies into a blender and blend on the highest setting until smooth in consistency.

14. Serve you meat with your gnocchi and your pureed veggie mixture. Garnish with your parmesan cheese and parsley and serve whenever you are ready.

(8) Creamy Cheesy Dumplings

This is a tasty side dish that you can easily make as a tasty side dish or to make a full lunch or dinner dish for yourself. The ingredients in this dish are incredibly versatile so feel free to add to add whatever ingredients you wish to make it truly delicious.

Serving Sizes: 8 Servings

Preparation Time: 2 Hours and 10 Minutes

List of Ingredients:

- 2 ¼ Cup of Cheese, Farmer Variety and Fresh
- ¼ Cup of Lard, Pork Variety
- 3 Eggs, Large in Size
- 1 Cup of Semolina
- Dash of Salt, For Taste

IIIIIIIIIIIIIIIIIIIIIIIIIIIIIIIIIIIIIIIIIIIIIIIIIIIIIII

Methods:

1. First mix together your eggs and lard until evenly mixed together.

2. Add your semolina and cheese into your mixture. Stir thoroughly to combine and cover with some plastic wrap. Set into your fridge to chill for the next 2 hours.

3. After this time heat up a large sized pot of water over medium heat until boiling.

4. Shape your mixture into even sized balls.

5. Carefully drop them into your boiling water and allow to boil until they begin to float to the surface. This should take at least 3 to 5 minutes.

6. Remove from the water and serve whenever you are ready. Enjoy.

(9) Croatian Style Stuffed Peppers

This is a dish that incorporates the natural sweetness of peppers to make a dish that you will want to make over and over. These peppers are absolutely delicious, filling and easy to make, I know you won't be able to get enough of it.

Serving Sizes: 4 Servings

Preparation Time: 2 Hours and 45 Minutes

Ingredients for Your Gravy:

- 4 Tablespoon of Tomato Puree
- 1 Liter of Vegetable Stock, Homemade Preferable
- ½ teaspoon of Vegeta
- 1 teaspoon of Savory Leaves, Fresh
- 2 teaspoon of Rosemary, Fresh
- 2 Tablespoon of Olive Oil, Extra Virgin Variety
- 1 Onion, Large in size and Finely Chopped
- 4 Cloves of Garlic, Smashed
- 4 Tablespoon of Flour, All Purpose Variety
- Dash of Salt and Pepper, For Taste

Ingredients for Your Stuffed Peppers:

- 4 Peppers, Sweet Variety and Medium in Size
- ½ Cup of Lentils, Uncooked Variety
- ½ Cup of Rice, Raw
- 1 Egg, Vegan Variety
- 2 Cloves of Garlic, Smashed
- 4 Tablespoon of Parsley, Roughly Chopped
- 1 Chili, Fresh, Red in Color, Seeded, Deveined and Finely Chopped
- 1 ½ Tablespoon of Paprika, Smoked
- 1 Tablespoon of Liquid Smoked
- ½ teaspoon of Black Pepper, For Taste
- Dash of Salt, For Taste

Remaining List of Ingredients:

- 2 Bay Leaves, Fresh
- 1 Stick of Celery, Fresh and Small in Size
- 1 Carrots, Fresh, Small in Size and Washed

Methods:

1. The first thing that you will want to do is cook your lentils. To do this first rinse and drain them. Place them into a large sized pan and add enough water to cover.

2. Set over medium heat and bring to a boil before reducing the heat to low. Cook for the next 20 minutes or until your lentils are tender to the touch. Once soft drain, rinse and set aside for later use.

3. Next make your gravy. To do this mix together your tomato, vegeta, savory leaves, fresh rosemary and your vegetable stock in a medium sized bowl until evenly mixed. Set aside for later use.

4. Then use a large sized skillet and add in your oil. Set over medium to high heat and once your oil is hot enough add in your onion. Cook until it begins to turn translucent.

5. Once translucent add in your garlic and cook until fragrant.

6. Add in your flour and continue to cook for an additional minute, making sure to stir continuously throughout this time.

7. Slowly add in your stock and stir until it comes to a boil and is thick in consistency. Once this season with some salt and pepper and remove from heat. Set aside for later use.

8. Next cut the tops off your peppers and set aside. Remove the seeds from your peppers and wash them thoroughly. Set aside for later use.

9. Then mix together your remaining ingredients for your stuffed peppers in a large sized bowl until thoroughly combined.

10. Scoop a spoonful or two of this stuffing into your peppers or until it is at least halfway full. Make sure that you do not overfill your peppers as the rice will swell as it cooks.

11. Place your stuffed peppers into a generously greased baking dish.

12. Pour your sauce over your peppers and top off each pepper with their lids.

13. Add in your fresh carrots, fresh celery, and fresh bay leaf.

14. Cover with some aluminum foil.

15. Heat your peppers over medium heat and bring it to a boil. Once boiling reduce the heat to low and allow to simmer for the next 2 hours.

16. After this time remove from heat and allow to cool for the next 10 to 15 minutes.

17. Serve your peppers with our mashed potatoes and gravy. Enjoy.

(10) Croatian Style Apple Pie Bars

Here is yet another sweet tasting dish that I know you are going to want to make over and over again. This dish is made out of crumbly butter dough and is packed full of sweet tasting cinnamon and apple filling, making it the perfect treat for the entire family can enjoy.

Serving Sizes: 3 Servings

Preparation Time: 1 Hour and 10 Minutes

List of Ingredients:

- 3 ¼ Cups of Flour, All Purpose Variety
- 1 teaspoon of Baker's Style Baking Powder
- 1 Egg, Large in Size
- ½ Cup of Sugar, White
- 1 ¾ Tablespoon of Butter, Soft
- 1 to 2 Tablespoon of Milk, Whole and Optional
- 2 Tablespoon of Bread Crumbs, Dried

Ingredients for Your Filling:

- 3 Pounds of Apples, Peeled, Cored and Thinly Sliced
- 3 Tablespoon of Sugar, White
- 1 teaspoon of Cinnamon, Ground

|||||||||||||||||||||||||||||||||||||||||||||||||||||||||

Methods:

1. The first thing that you will want to do is make your dough. To do this use a large sized bowl and add in your flour, baker's style baking powder, large egg, white sugar and soft butter. Stir thoroughly to mix or until a dough begins to form.

2. Add in at least a spoonful of milk if your dough is too dry. Knead it for at least 5 minutes before wrapping in some plastic wrap and placing into your fridge to rest for the next 30 minutes.

3. While your dough is resting make your filling. To do this mix together all of your ingredients for your filling in a large sized bowl until evenly mixed.

4. Next divide your dough into two equal sized pieces and roll out onto a floured surface to form a large sized square. Press one piece of your rolled out dough into a large sized pie pan, making sure to stretch the dough up the sides.

5. Sprinkle your dough with bread crumbs and spoon your filling right into the center.

6. Top off with your second rolled out piece of dough.

7. Place into your oven to bake for the next 45 minutes at 350 degrees or until your pie crust is golden in color.

8. After this time remove from your oven and sprinkle your powdered sugar over the top. Serve while warm and enjoy.

(11) Croatian Style Bean Stew

If you are looking for an authentic and absolutely delicious dish to enjoy, you can't go wrong with his recipe. This is a great dish to make during the cold winter months or whenever you are looking for something a little more filling.

Serving Sizes: 6 to 8 Servings

Preparation Time: 35 Minutes

List of Ingredients:

- 1 ½ Cups of Beans, Borlotti Variety and Soaked
- 8 ½ Cups of Water, Cold
- 2 ¼ Cups of Bacon, Bones Variety
- ½ Cup of Celery, Fresh and Finely Chopped
- ¼ Cup of Capsicum, Red in Color and Finely Chopped
- ¼ Cup of Oil, Extra Virgin Variety
- 4 Cloves of Garlic, Finely Chopped
- 1 Tablespoon of Paprika
- 1 Tablespoon of Flour, All Purpose Variety
- Dash of Parsley, Fresh and for Garnish

- Dash of Olive Oil, Extra Virgin Variety and for Garnish

IIIIIIIIIIIIIIIIIIIIIIIIIIIIIIIIIIIIIIIIIIIIIIIIIIIIIIIIII

Methods:

1. First use a large sized saucepan and add in your bacon, water, borlotti beans, red capsicum, bay leaves and onions. Stir thoroughly to combine and set over medium heat.

2. Bring this mixture to a boil and reduce the heat to low. Allow to simmer for the next hour or until your beans are soft to the touch.

3. Next use a small sized pan and add in your oil. Once the oil is hot enough add in your garlic and cook over low heat until gold in color. Once gold remove from your pan and set aside for later use.

4. Next add in your paprika and flour. Stir thoroughly to combine and continue to simmer for at least one minute to form a roux. Once your roux has formed add your garlic back into it.

5. Remove the bacon bones from your cooked beans and add your beans to your paprika mixture. Stir thoroughly to combine.

6. Allow to simmer for the next 5 minutes before removing from heat.

7. Serve and garnish your dish with your parsley and olive oil. For the tastiest results, serve with some fresh bread.

(12) Croatian Style Dumplings

These delicious dumplings are made out of mashed potato dough, which makes for a delicious lunch or dessert dish, regardless of what you make this treat for. Regardless I know you are going to love it.

Serving Sizes: 16 Servings

Preparation Time: 50 Minutes

List of Ingredients:

- 3 Potatoes, Medium in Size, Peeled, Boiled, Mashed and Cooled
- 2 Eggs, Large in Size and Beaten
- ½ teaspoon of Salt, For Taste
- 1 ½ Cups of Flour, All Purpose Variety
- 16 Plums, Italian Prune Variety, Washed and Pitted
- 16 Sugar Cubes
- 4 Tablespoon of Butter, Soft
- ¼ Cup of Bread Crumbs, Italian Variety
- Dash of Sugar, Confectioner's Variety
- Dash of Cinnamon, Ground Variety

Methods:

1. First use a large sized bowl and mix together your potatoes, eggs and dash of salt until thoroughly combined.

2. Add in your flour and continue to mix until a soft dough begins to form.

3. Place a sugar cube into the center of each of your plums and place into a large sized pot of salted water. Bring to a boil.

4. Next place some flour on your hands and flatten out a small portion of your dough.

5. Place a plum right into the center of it and fold the sides over to enclose it completely.

6. Carefully drop into some boiling water and cook for the next 20 minutes. Repeat until all of your dough has been boiled.

7. While you are boiling your dough, melt your butter in a large sized skillet. Once your butter is melted add in your breadcrumbs and cook until brown in color.

8. Transfer your dumplings to a large sized serving plate and pour your breadcrumbs over your dumplings.

9. Dust with your sugar and cinnamon and serve. Enjoy.

(13) Classic Croatian Style Kale Pie

Now this is a dish that you are going to want to make if you are looking for the very heart of Croatian food. It is an incredibly delicious dish to enjoy and is great to enjoy as a tasty snack or whenever you need to spoil yourself.

Serving Sizes: 4 to 6 Servings

Preparation Time: 1 Hour and 40 Minutes

Ingredients for Your Dough:

- 2 Cups of Flour, All Purpose Variety
- 1 Tablespoon of Olive Oil, Extra Virgin Variety
- Dash of Salt and Pepper, For Taste
- 2/3 Cup of Water, Cold

Ingredients for Your Filling:

- 1 Handful of Kale, Fresh
- 1 Onion, Large in Size and Finely Diced
- 3 Cloves of Garlic, Minced
- 4 Tablespoon of Parsley, Fresh and Roughly Chopped
- 1 Tablespoon of Olive Oil, Extra Virgin Variety

- Dash of Salt and Pepper, For Taste
- Dash of Olive Oil, Extra Virgin Variety and Optional

||||||||||||||||||||||||||||||||||||||||||||||||||||

Methods:

1. First add in your flour, dash of olive oil and dash of salt and pepper into a large sized mixing bowl.

2. Then slowly add in your water and stir thoroughly to combine. Knead your dough as it forms to make it come together.

3. Knead your dough for at least 5 minutes or until it is elastic in texture.

4. Place into a large sized oiled bowl and cover. Allow to rest for the next hour.

5. Prepare your filling next. To do this chop your kale leaves finely and add to a large sized bowl.

6. Add in your onion, garlic and parsley. Toss to combine before adding in a dash of salt and pepper and your olive oil. Toss again to incorporate. Set aside for later use.

7. After this time transfer your dough to a lightly floured surface. Divide your dough in two and roll to a large sized rectangle. Transfer this dough into your baking dish and add in your kale filling.

8. Roll out your second piece of dough the same way and place on top of your kale filling.

9. Seal the edges and make a few holes in the top using a fork.

10. Place into your oven to bake at 375 degrees for the next 20 minutes or until light brown in color.

11. After this time remove and serve while still piping hot. Enjoy!

(14) Croatian Style Summer Time Cucumber Salad

Just as the name implies this is a delicious summer time salad recipe that you can make if you are looking for a healthy dish to enjoy. It is easy to put together and will leave your feeling satisfied.

Serving Sizes: 1 Serving

Preparation Time: 1 Hour

List of Ingredients:

- ¾ Cup of Cucumbers, Fresh and Thinly Sliced
- 1 Clove of Garlic, Finely Chopped
- 1 Tablespoon of Vinegar, Wine Variety
- Dash of Salt and Pepper, For Taste
- Dash of Chile Pepper, Optional and for Taste
- 1 Tablespoon of Olive Oil, Extra Virgin Variety
- 3 Tablespoon of Water, Warm

IIIIIIIIIIIIIIIIIIIIIIIIIIIIIIIIIIIIIIIIIIIIIIIIIIII

Methods:

1. First peel and thinly slice your cucumbers. Place into a large sized bowl.

2. Add in your garlic and toss thoroughly to combine.

3. Then add in your vinegar, olive oil and water.

4. Season with a dash of salt and pepper. Season with your chili if you are using it. Toss thoroughly to combine.

5. Place into your fridge to chill for the next hour before serving. Enjoy.

(15) Croatian Style Swiss Chard and Potatoes

Here is yet another healthy Croatian style dish that I know you won't be able to get enough of. It is a great recipe to enjoy if you are looking to lose weight or if you are looking for something on the healthier side.

Serving Sizes: 2 Servings

Preparation Time: 30 Minutes

List of Ingredients:

- 2 Potatoes, Peeled, Large in Size and Finely Diced
- 1 Bunch of Swiss Chard, Fresh, Washed, Stems Removed and Roughly Chopped
- 1 Clove of Garlic, Minced
- 4 Tablespoon of Olive Oil, Extra Virgin Variety
- Dash of Sea Salt, For Taste

IIIIIIIIIIIIIIIIIIIIIIIIIIIIIIIIIIIIIIIIIIIIIIIIIIII

Methods:

1. The first thing that you will want to do is boil your potatoes in a large sized pot filled with water until soft to the touch. Once soft, drain and set the potatoes aside.

2. Then boil your Swiss chard next for the next 3 minutes or until wilted. Once wilted drain and place onto a large sized serving plate.

3. Then use a small sized bowl and mix together your garlic, olive oil and dash of sea salt. Stir thoroughly to combine.

4. Pour your oil mixture over your Chard and toss thoroughly to coat.

5. Add in your potatoes and toss again to combine.

6. Serve right away and enjoy.

(16) Delicious Govedi Smotucljci

Here is a tasty and delicious dinner meal that you can make if you are looking for something on the fancier side. It is incredibly easy to make to make and packed full of delicious flavor, I know you won't be able to resist it.

Serving Sizes: 4 Servings

Preparation Time: 25 Minutes

List of Ingredients:

- 2 ½ Cups of Veal, Rump Variety
- 4 Tablespoon of Onion, Finely Chopped
- 4 Tablespoon of Bacon, Finely Chopped
- 2 Tablespoon of Cornichons, Finely Chopped

Ingredients for Your Sauce:

- 1 ½ Onions, Finely Chopped
- ½ of Capsicum, Red in Color and Finely Chopped
- 1 Stick of Celery, Fresh and Finely Chopped
- 2 Cloves of Garlic, Freshly Grated
- 1 ½ Tablespoon of Flour, All Purpose Variety
- 3 Cups of Water, Warm
- 1 teaspoon of Vegeta
- Dash of Black Pepper, For Taste
- ¼ Cup of Parsley, Fresh and Roughly Chopped

||||||||||||||||||||||||||||||||||||||||||||||||||

Methods:

1. The first thing that you will want to do is pound your veal into 3-inch thickness and cut into 12 equal sized pieces. Season each veal slice with a dash of salt and pepper. Set aside for later use.

2. Then use a small sized bowl and thoroughly combine your onion, bacon and cornichon until thoroughly mixed.

3. Sprinkle your mixture over the ends of each veal and roll into a cigar like shape. Use toothpicks to secure it in place.

4. Next heat up a large sized skillet placed over medium to high heat. Add in some oil and once the oil is hot enough sear your veal rolls. Remove and set aside for later use.

5. Add some more oil to your pan and once it is hot enough add in your onions, red capsicum, fresh celery and minced garlic until soft to the touch.

6. Then add in your flour and mix again to thoroughly combine.

7. Add in your water, vegeta and dash of pepper. Stir to incorporate before returning your veal rolls to your pan.

8. Reduce the heat to low and allow to simmer in your sauce for the next 15 to 20 minutes, making sure to turn at least once.

9. Remove from heat and serve with a garnish of fresh parsley. Enjoy right away.

(17) Traditional Cheese Strukli

Now here is a classic and traditional Croatian dish that I know you won't be able to get enough of. This is a traditional dish that is served up in many popular Croatian restaurants and I know it will become an instant hit in your household.

Serving Sizes: 8 to 10 Servings

Preparation Time: 55 Minutes

List of Ingredients:

- 5 1/3 Cups of Flour, All Purpose Variety
- 5 Eggs, Large in Size and Beaten
- 1 Tablespoon of Oil, Cooking Variety
- Dash of Salt, For Taste
- 2 ½ Pounds of Cottage Cheese, Dried and Curd
- 1 Cup of Butter, Fully Melted
- 4 Cups of Heavy Cream

||||||||||||||||||||||||||||||||||||||||||||||||||||

Methods:

1. Use a large sized mixing bowl and make your dough. To do this add in your flour, 1 egg, touch of oil and some water mixed with salt into it. Stir to thoroughly combine until a dough forms. Knead your dough in your bowl until smooth to the touch.

2. Spray your dough with some cooking spray and allow to rest for the next 15 minutes.

3. Make your filling. To do this mix your cheese with your 4 remaining eggs in a medium sized mixing bowl.

4. Season with a touch of salt and add in at least ½ cup of your butter. Blend until smooth in consistency.

5. Sprinkle some flour onto a flat surface and roll out your dough until paper thin.

6. Spread your cheese mixture over the top and brush the sough with some melted butter.

7. Roll your dough jelly roll style and cut into 20 equal sized pieces.

8. Boil your dough in some boiling water for the next 10 minutes. After this time drain and place into a large sized baking dish.

9. Preheat your oven to 200 degrees. While your oven is heating up pour your remaining butter over your dough and top off with your heavy cream.

10. Place into your oven to bake for the next 20 to 30 minutes or until golden in color.

11. After this time remove and set aside to cool before serving. Enjoy.

(18) Hearty Bean and Pasta Soup

Here is yet another hearty and delicious soup recipe you can enjoy whenever you have a craving for something more on the filling side. For the tastiest results I highly recommend serving this dish with some bread.

Serving Sizes: 2 Servings

Preparation Time: 45 Minutes

List of Ingredients:

- 1 ½ Cups of Beans, White and Dried Variety
- ½ Cup of Pork Bones, Smoked Variety
- 3 Sausages, Kranski Variety
- 21 Cups of Water, Warm
- 2 Carrots, Fresh and Cut into Small Sized Pieces
- 2 Potatoes, Medium in Size and Cut into Small Sized Pieces
- Dash of Olive Oil, Extra Virgin Variety
- 1 Onion, Large in Size and Finely Diced
- ½ Cup of Pancetta, Chopped Coarsely
- 1 teaspoon of Paprika, Smoked Variety
- 4 Cloves of Garlic, Diced

- ¼ Bunch of Parsley, Fresh and Diced Finely
- 1 teaspoon of Tomato Paste
- ¼ Cup of Pasta, Shelled Variety
- Dash of Salt and Pepper, For Taste

||||||||||||||||||||||||||||||||||||||||||||||||||

Methods:

1. The first thing that you will want to do is place your beans into a large sized bowl to soak overnight.

2. The next day place some olive oil in a large sized pot and set over medium heat.

3. Once the oil is hot enough add in your onions and pancetta. Cook until your onions begin to turn translucent.

4. Add in soaked beans after they have been strained and add in your bones and sausage. Stir thoroughly to combine.

5. Next fill up your pot with water and cook over medium heat for the next 30 minutes.

6. Add in your potatoes, fresh carrots, diced garlic, fresh parsley, tomato paste and dash of paprika. Stir again to combine.

7. Continue to cook over medium heat until soft to the touch.

8. Then add in your pasta. Toss to thoroughly combine.

9. Season with a dash of salt and pepper.

10. Remove from heat and serve whenever you are ready.

(19) Croatian Style Cabbage Rolls

Looking for a healthy treat to enjoy guilt free? Then this is the perfect dish for you to make. This is yet another traditional Croatian recipe that has been passed down through my family for generations and once you get a taste of it yourself, you will see why that is.

Serving Sizes: 8 to 10 Servings

Preparation Time: 2 to 3 Hours

List of Ingredients:

- 2 Cups of Veal, Minced
- 2 Cups of Pork, Minced
- 1 Egg, Large in Size
- 1 Onion, Medium in Size and Chopped Finely
- 2 Tablespoon of Oil, Vegetable Variety
- 1 teaspoon of Paprika
- 1 teaspoon of Salt, For Taste
- Dash of Ground Pepper, For Taste
- 1 ½ Tablespoon of Paprika
- ½ Cup of Water, Warm
- 2 Tablespoon of Rice

- ¾ Cup of Bacon Bones, Smoked Variety
- 3 ¾ Cup of Sauerkraut, Drained
- 10 Cabbage Leaves, Fresh, Pickled and Drained
- 3 Tablespoon of Olive Oil, Extra Virgin Variety
- 3 Tablespoon + 1 Tablespoon of Paprika
- 2 Cups of Water, Warm
- 1 teaspoon of Vegeta
- Some Parsley, Flat Leaf Variety, Finely Chopped and for Garnish

||||||||||||||||||||||||||||||||||||||||||||||||||||||

Methods:

1. Use a large sized bowl and add in your minced meat, paprika, onion and dash of salt and pepper. Stir thoroughly to combine.

2. Then rinse out your rice in some water, until the water begins to run clear. Make sure that you leave at least 2 tablespoons of water in it.

3. Add your rice to your mince mixture and stir thoroughly to combine. Set this mixture aside.

4. Next place your bacon bones into a small sized bowl and cover with enough water. Set aside to soak.

5. Pour your onion mixture into a large sized baking dish. Add your sauerkraut to the top and spread evenly.

6. Form your meat mixture into even sized patties and place into the center of your cabbage leaves. Fold and place this rolls into your baking dish.

7. Prick each of your rolls with a knife and tuck your soaked bacon bones into each one.

8. Spread your remaining sauerkraut over the top and place into your fridge to chill overnight.

9. The next day preheat your oven to 350 degrees.

10. While your oven is heating up use a large sized skillet and heat up your oil over medium heat. Once your oil is hot enough add in your flour and paprika into it to form a roux.

11. Once a roux has formed add at least 2 cups of water into it along with your Vegeta and stir thoroughly for the next 5 minutes as it cooks over low heat. After this time remove from heat and pour over your mixture in your baking dish.

12. Place your dish into your oven to bake for the next 2 to 3 hours or until golden brown on all sides.

13. After this time remove from your oven and serve with a garnish of fresh parsley while it is still piping hot.

(20) Croatian Style Chocolate Layered Cake

This is a dessert dish that you can make if you are looking for the most decadent late-night treat to enjoy. It is absolutely the best, especially if you have a strong sweet tooth that needs to be satisfied.

Serving Sizes: 4 Servings

Preparation Time: 1 Hour

Ingredients for The Cake Layers:

- 2 ½ Cups of Flour, All Purpose Variety
- ½ teaspoon of Baker's Style Baking Powder
- 2 Eggs, Whites Only
- ¾ Cup of Cream, Heavy Variety
- ½ Cup of Sugar, White
- ¾ Cup of Butter, Soft

Ingredients for Your Filling:

- 4 ¼ Cup of Milk, Whole
- ½ Cup of Butter, Soft
- ¾ Cup of Sugar, White
- ¾ Cup of Chocolate, Your Favorite Kind
- 5 Tablespoon of Flour, All Purpose Variety
- 1 teaspoon of Vanilla, Pure

Ingredients for Your Glaze:

- ¾ Cup of Chocolate, Your Favorite Kind
- 3 Tablespoon of Olive Oil, Extra Virgin Variety
- ¼ Cup of Butter, Soft

IIIIIIIIIIIIIIIIIIIIIIIIIIIIIIIIIIIIIIIIIIIIIIIIIIII

Methods:

1. The first thing that you will want to do is make your cake filling. To do this cook up your milk with your vanilla and sugar in a large sized saucepan until it begins to boil. Once it is boiling whisk your flour and milk together in a separate bowl until evenly mixed.

2. Pour this mixture into your boiling milk and continue to whisk to thoroughly combine.

3. Reduce the heat to low and add in your chocolate. Stir constantly until your chocolate begins to melt and your mixture begins to become thick in consistency. Remove from heat.

4. Add in your butter and stir thoroughly to combine. Set aside and allow to cool completely.

5. Next preheat your oven to 350 degrees.

6. While your oven is heating up make your dough. To do this beat together your butter, sugar, whites of your eggs and cream in a medium sized bowl until evenly mixed.

7. Then add in your flour and baking powder. Knead with your hands until a dough begins to form.

8. Separate your dough into five equal sized pieces and roll out each piece into a small sized rectangle, making sure they are as thin as possible. Once rolled out place your rectangles onto a large sized baking tray.

9. Place your cake layers into your oven to bake one-by-one for the next 8 to 9 minutes or until light in color. Once baked remove and allow to cool completely.

10. Next make your glaze. To do this mix together your butter, chocolate and olive oil in a pot set over some boiling water. Once your mixture is fully melted and evenly combined, remove from heat and set aside for later use.

11. Assemble your cake. To do this place one layer of your cooked dough onto a baking sheet and spread your filling over it. Cover with another layer of cooked dough and add yet another layer of filling. Repeat until your cooked dough and filling has been used.

12. Top off your cake with your glaze and set into your fridge to set overnight.

13. The next day cut your cake into small sized pieces and serve while cold. Enjoy.

(21) Traditional Pasticada

If there is one dish that is considered to be "famous" in Croatian cuisine, it is this one. This dish makes meat incredibly tender and is one of the most filling and delicious Croatian dishes you will ever come across.

Serving Sizes: 4 Servings

Preparation Time: 50 Minutes

List of Ingredients:

- 1 Beef Round, Large in Size
- 4 Onions, Medium in Size and Thinly Sliced
- 3 Cloves of Garlic, Thinly Sliced
- 1 Root of Celery, Fresh and Grated
- 2 Carrots, Fresh and Grated
- 1 teaspoon of Sugar, White
- 6 Cloves, Whole
- ½ Cup of Pancetta, Thinly Sliced
- ¾ Cup of Vinegar, Red Wine Variety
- ½ Cup of Olive Oil, Extra Virgin Variety
- 1 ¼ Cup of Beef Broth, Homemade Preferable
- ¾ Cup of Red Wine, Your Favorite kind

- ¾ Cup of Prosek
- ½ Cup of Raisins, Your Favorite Kind
- 6 Prunes, Fresh
- ½ teaspoon of Nutmeg, Ground
- 1 teaspoon of Tomato Puree

|||||||||||||||||||||||||||||||||||||||||||||||||||||

Methods:

1. The first thing that you will want to do is make a few small sized cuts all over your beef. In these slices add in your garlic and pancetta.

2. Do the same with your cloves and place your meat into a large sized ceramic bowl.

3. Pour in your vinegar and water into this bowl. Cover and place into your fridge to marinate overnight.

4. The next day remove your meat from the marinade and set aside for later use.

5. Next pour your oil in a large sized frying pan and heat over medium heat. Once it is hot enough add in your onions, fresh carrots, fresh celery and white sugar. Stir thoroughly and cook until soft to the touch.

6. Once your vegetables are tender to the touch add in your meat and continue to cook until brown in color.

7. Add in your broth and allow to simmer over low heat for the next 2 hours.

8. After this time add in your favorite kind of raisins, ground nutmeg, red wine and prosek. Bring your mixture to a boil.

9. Remove your meat from your pan and cut into small sized pieces. Return back to your pan and add in your pureed tomato.

10. Bring this mixture to a boil again.

11. Remove from heat and serve with some gnocchi. Enjoy!

(22)   Traditional Raznjici

This is yet another simple, yet delicious dish that even the pickiest eaters in your household are going to fall in love with. This is a great dish to make for lunch or for dinner. Either way I know you are going to love it.

Serving Sizes: 4 Servings

Preparation Time: 6 Hours and 25 Minutes

List of Ingredients:

- ½ Cup of Oil, Vegetable Variety
- ¼ Cup of Vinegar, Red Wine Variety
- 1 Onion, Thinly Sliced
- 4 Clove of Garlic, Sliced
- 3 Bay Leaves, Fresh
- 2 teaspoons of Salt, For Taste
- ½ teaspoon of Oregano, Fresh
- ¼ teaspoon of Black Pepper, For Taste
- 2 Pounds of Pork Loin, Cut into Small Sized Pieces

||||||||||||||||||||||||||||||||||||||||||||||||||||

Methods:

1. The first thing that you will want to do is mix everything together except for your pork in a large sized bowl to make your marinade.

2. Trim your pork of any fat and cut into small sized cubes.

3. Add your pork to your marinade and toss thoroughly to coat.

4. Cover with some plastic wrap and place into your fridge to marinate overnight.

5. After this time place your pork onto your skewers and preheat a grill to high heat.

6. Once your grill is hot enough add your pork onto it and grill for at least 10 to 20 minutes.

7. Remove from your grill and serve while still piping hot. Enjoy!

(23)　Croatian Style Walnut Bread

This is a delicious bread recipe that you can make if you are looking for the perfect way to satisfy your strongest sweet tooth. This traditional European dessert bread is especially delicious if you serve it with a steaming cup of coffee.

Serving Sizes: 6 Servings

Preparation Time: 3 Hours

Ingredients for Your Dough:

- ½ teaspoon of Sugar, White
- ¼ teaspoon of Flour, All Purpose Variety
- 2 Tablespoon of Water, Warm
- 1 ½ teaspoon of Yeast, Dry
- ½ Cup of Milk, 2% Variety
- 3 Tablespoon of Sugar, White
- ¾ teaspoon of Salt, For Taste
- 1 Egg, Large in Size and Beaten
- ½ of a Vanilla bean, Scraped Variety
- 1 Tablespoon of Butter, Unsalted Variety and Fully Melted
- 2 Cups of Flour, All Purpose Variety

Ingredients for Your Topping:

- 1 Egg White, Beaten
- 1 ½ teaspoon of Sugar, Granulated Variety
- 1 Tablespoon of Butter, Fully Melted

Ingredients for Your Filling:

- 1 ¾ Cups of Walnuts, Ground variety
- ¼ Cup of Milk, 2% Variety
- 1 Egg Yolk, Beaten
- ½ of a Vanilla Bean, Scraped Variety
- ½ Cup of Sugar, White
- 2 Tablespoon of Cocoa, Powdered Variety and Unsweetened Variety

IIIIIIIIIIIIIIIIIIIIIIIIIIIIIIIIIIIIIIIIIIIIIIIIIII

Methods:

1. The first thing that you will want to do is activate your yeast. To do this use a small sized bowl and stir together your sugar, flour and yeast until evenly mixed.

2. Pour in your water and stir again until your yeast dissolves. Allow to stand for the next 5 minutes to activate the yeast.

3. Next make your dough. To do this use a medium sized saucepan and heat up your milk until it begins to boil. Make sure that you stir constantly as it begins to boil. Remove from heat and pour into a large sized bowl.

4. In the same bowl add in your sugar and salt and stir thoroughly to combine.

5. Add in your eggs, yeast mixture, melted butter and flour. Stir thoroughly to incorporate.

6. Turn your dough onto a lightly floured surface and knead for the next 5 minutes or until smooth to the touch. Place into a lightly greased bowl and cover with some plastic wrap. Allow to sit in a warm place until it doubles in size.

7. While your dough is rising, make your filling. To do this use a large sized bowl and mix together your walnuts, sugar and powdered cocoa.

8. Heat up your remaining milk in a large sized saucepan placed over medium heat. Add in your butter and continue to heat up until your mixture is boiling. Pour this mixture over your nut and sugar mixture and stir thoroughly to combine.

9. Add in your egg yolk and vanilla and stir again to combine. Allow to sit for a few minutes or until thick in consistency.

10. Next sprinkle some flour over a flat surface. Place your dough on top and roll out your dough until it is at least a large sized square.

11. Place at least 1 to 2 spoonfuls of your melted butter over the top of the dough. Then spoon your filling over your dough and spread it easily over the surface.

12. Roll your dough jelly roll style and brush the surface with some egg white. Top off with some granulated sugar.

13. Place your roll into a large sized baking dish and cover with some plastic wrap. Allow to rest for the next 15 minutes.

14. While your dough is resting preheat your oven to 350 degrees. Once it is hot add in your dough into your oven to bake for the next 45 minutes or until completely baked through.

15. After this time remove your dough from the oven and spread your melted butter over the top. Place onto a wire rack to cool for the next 20 minutes. Serve whenever you are ready.

(24)   Croatian Style Almond Cookies

These naturally gluten free cookie recipe is another recipe you will want to make if you wish to satisfy those picky eaters in your household. They are crispy on the outside while moist on the inside. I know you are going to fall in love with these cookies.

Serving Sizes: 24 Servings

Preparation Time: 20 Minutes

List of Ingredients:

- 2 Cups of Flour, Almond Variety
- 1 Cup of Sugar, White
- 2 Oranges, Fresh and Zest Only
- 2 Egg Whites, beaten
- ½ Cup of Almond, Chopped Coarsely

||||||||||||||||||||||||||||||||||||||||||||||||||||||

Methods:

1. The first thing that you will want to do is preheat your oven to 350 degrees. While your oven is heating up line a baking sheet with some parchment paper. Set aside for later use.

2. Next use a large sized bowl and add in your flour, fresh orange zest, white sugar and beaten egg whites. Stir thoroughly until moist to the touch.

3. Place your chopped nuts onto a large sized plate.

4. Take tablespoon sized balls of your dough and shape them into footballs. Roll into your chopped almonds, making sure to press lightly as you do so.

5. Place your cookies onto your baking sheet.

6. Place into your oven to bake for the next 10 to 12 minutes or until golden in color.

7. After this time remove from your oven and allow to cool slightly before serving. Enjoy.

(25)   Tasty Jam Crescent Cookies

These delicious treats are melt in your mouth delicious and are packed full of your favorite jam. This is the perfect cookies to make whenever you are looking for something to satisfy your strongest sweet tooth.

Serving Sizes: 10 Servings

Preparation Time: 25 Minutes

List of Ingredients:

- 3 2/3 Cups of Flour, pastry Variety
- 1 ½ teaspoon of Baker's Style Baking Powder
- 2 Sticks + 5 teaspoon of Butter, Melted
- 2/3 Cup + 3 Tablespoon of Sour Cream
- 1 Tablespoon of Sugar Powdered Variety
- ½ teaspoon of Lemon, Zest Only
- Dash of Salt

Ingredients for Your Filling:

- 1 ½ Cup of Jam, Your Favorite Kind
- Some Powdered Sugar, For Dusting

||||||||||||||||||||||||||||||||||||||||||||||||||

Methods:

1. First mix together your flour, baker's style baking powder, melted butter, sour cream, fresh lemon zest, dash of salt and powdered sugar together in a large sized bowl until evenly mixed.

2. Once a dough begins to form wrap your dough in some plastic wrap and place into your fridge to chill for at least one hour.

3. Place your dough onto a lightly floured surface and roll out into a thin sized circle.

4. Cut your circle into 6 equal sized triangles.

5. Spoon at least a spoonful of jam in each triangle and roll into crescents.

6. Place your cookies onto a baking sheet and place into your oven to bake at 350 degrees for the next 15 minutes.

7. After this time remove your cookies from the oven and dust them with some powdered sugar. Serve once slightly cool.

About the Author

Nancy Silverman is an accomplished chef and cookbook author from Essex, Vermont. She attended Essex High School where she graduated with honors then moved on to University of Vermont where she received a degree in Nutrition and Food Sciences. She later attended New England Culinary Institute located close to her home town of Essex, in Montpelier, Vermont.

Nancy met her husband at school in Vermont when the two were set up on a date by a mutual friend. Both shared a love of the culinary arts and it was love at first sight! Nancy and Dennis have been married for 16 years and live on a beautiful property close to Nancy's childhood home in Essex. They have 3 children and 2 golden retrievers named Lucy and Ricky.

Nancy loves growing her own vegetables and herbs in the garden she has cultivated and cared for in the family's spacious backyard. Her greatest joy is cooking in her modern kitchen with her family and creating inspiring and delicious meals. She often says that she has perfected her signature dishes based on her family's critique of each and every one.

Nancy has her own catering company and has also been fortunate enough to be head chef at some of Vermont's most exclusive restaurants. She aspires to open her own restaurant, but for now she is content working from home and building her catering empire with the help of her children. When a friend suggested she share some of her outstanding signature dishes, she decided to add cookbook author to her repertoire of personal achievements. Being a technological savvy woman, she felt the e-book realm would be a better fit and soon she had her first cookbook available online. As of today, Nancy has sold over 1,000 e-books and has shared her culinary experiences and brilliant recipes with people from all over the world! She plans on expanding into self-help books and dietary cookbooks, so stayed tuned!

Author's Afterthoughts

Thank you for making the decision to invest in one of my cookbooks! I cherish all my readers and hope you find joy in preparing these meals as I have.

There are so many books available and I am truly grateful that you decided to buy this one and follow it from beginning to end.

I love hearing from my readers on what they thought of this book and any value they received from reading it. As a personal favor, I would appreciate any feedback you can give in the form of a review on Amazon and please be honest! This kind of support will help others make an informed choice on and will help me tremendously in producing the best quality books possible.

My most heartfelt thanks,

Nancy Silverman

If you're interested in more of my books, be sure to follow my author page on Amazon (can be found on the link Bellow) or scan the QR-Code.

https://www.amazon.com/author/nancy-silverman

Made in the USA
Coppell, TX
03 November 2020

40739159R00059